AVOCADO

THE GOODNESS OF AVOCADO

40 DELICIOUS
HEALTH-BOOSTING
RECIPES

LUCY JESSOP
PHOTOGRAPHY BY CLARE WINFIELD

KYLE BOOKS

CONTENTS

AVO ADORATION

**I love avocados, you love avocados,
we all love avocados—but why?**

When I crave avocado, nothing else will do. It is unique.
Unlike most other fruit, vegetables, and salad leaves,
avocado can't easily be substituted—its rich, velvety
smoothness and creamy, mild grassy flavor is matchless.
Avo brings something special to a recipe that nothing
else can; something virtuous and indulgent, all rolled
into one. It is also endlessly versatile, simple and quick
to prepare and insanely nutritious.

My recipes aim to celebrate the deliciousness of
the avocado and show off its true potential, while
remaining easy to make and on the whole very
healthy. Here, avocado not only brings an added layer
of indulgence (and nutrients) to old time favorites—
it also transforms typically decadent dishes into
healthier, cleaner alternatives.

Above all, these are recipes for real life, ranging from
quick and nourishing weekday suppers, hearty, fill-
you-up salads and revitalizing smoothies, snacks, and
lunches to holiday brunches, easy summer party food,
and more wholesome sweet treats.

WONDROUS WAYS

With avocados there are no rules; it really is the most versatile ingredient I've ever cooked with, both for flavor and in the many wondrous ways it can be prepared. Mashed, whizzed, sliced, baked, griddled, frozen, you name it, the avocado shines in all these glorious guises. These recipes are divided into four chapters—based on the way you want to prepare your avocado: blended, smashed, chopped, and sweet.

In the **Blended** chapter you'll find silky smooth salad dressings and soups, addictive pesto, luscious dips for dunking crunchy crudités or sweet potato chips, and nutritious smoothies.

The **Smashed** chapter brings you guacamole, plus twists on the classic to slather on toast, top with eggs, or scoop up with pita or chips.

Avocados are diced and sliced as well as pickled, griddled and battered in the **Chopped** chapter—there are salsas, mouth-watering ceviches, and summery suppers to boot.

Finally, the **Sweet** chapter reveals the surprising potential of the avocado, showing how it can replace butter, cream and even eggs to make delicious yet healthier treats.

If there are countless ways to prepare avocado, there is even more scope with flavor in play. Distinctive in its velvety texture, yet rich, creamy, mild and mellow in flavor, it is amazingly adaptable. Avocado calms and soothes where there's heat from chili peppers or fiery ginger, it balances zingy citrus and aromatic herbs, welcomes delicate spices, stands up to smoked fish or salty cheese, and its green, grassy, earthiness pairs seamlessly with all manner of vegetables, nuts, grains, and seeds.

With every country enjoying its own delicious way of devouring avocado, these recipes are inspired by global flavors, taking their cue all the way from the avo's native Central America to Japan, the Middle East, Thailand, Spain, France, Italy, Scandinavia, and more.

ALL ABOUT THE AVO

The avocado tree is native to Central America and Mexico and has been grown there and in South America for thousands of years. There are hundreds of varieties of avocado, but today only a handful of these are farmed for commercial export—they're grown everywhere from Mexico, Chile, and Peru to California, South Africa, and New Zealand.

Common varieties range from the pear shaped, smooth, green-skinned Fuerte, to rounder fruits such as the Reed and the popular pebbly skinned Hass. Others come in varying shapes and sizes—look out for Bacon, Lamb Hass, Pinkerton, Gwen, and Zutano.

A NOTE ON HEALTHY EATING

For me, flavor is the only answer to healthy eating and is always top of my list when I create a recipe. With loads of flavor comes satisfaction, which leaves little need (or room) for anything too unhealthy.

None of these recipes have been shoe-horned in for the sake of being healthy. Quite a few happen to be vegetarian, or are easily adapted to be so, and a good number are suitable for those avoiding gluten and dairy. Avocado equals goodness, therefore each recipe is by default nourishing and balanced. Many are naturally virtuous, being based on fresh vegetables, whole grains and few processed ingredients, most of them are extremely good for you and one or two are once-in-a-while treats to be savored.

Mashed on toast with a pinch of sea salt and a squeeze of lime—it's the sense of luxury avocado brings to even the simplest of dishes which makes healthy eating a delight, not a chore, and the reason so many of us love avo. And I hope that's what all of the recipes in this book are—food to brighten your day while making you feel good, recipes you'll make over and over, share with family and pass onto friends. I hope you'll enjoy them as much as I have loved creating them.

NUTRITION IN A NUTSHELL

The term "superfood" is often overused, but for the avocado it's a deserved and well earned title. Avocados provide nearly 20 vitamins and minerals, including noteworthy amounts of fibre, good fats, folic acid, vitamin E, and potassium.

There's no denying avocados are high in fat (and therefore calories), but that shouldn't put you off, because it's the good kind, monounsaturated fat, which has been found to help lower cholesterol levels and maintain a healthy weight. This sort of fat also improves the absorption of fat soluble vitamins A, D, E and K. In baking and desserts, avocado can offer a healthier alternative to butter or cream, which omits the need for dairy (therefore suitable for those who are intolerant) and also instantly cuts the overall saturated fat level.

♦ Vitamin E is a powerful antioxidant, which can help reduce the risk of chronic health conditions like heart disease and also protect the body's cells against damaging free radicals—overall it's important for keeping skin, eyes, and the immune system healthy.

♦ Avocado is also a useful source of potassium (containing even more than bananas), which helps to balance sodium in the diet and maintain healthy blood pressure.

♦ Folic acid is another of avocado's vitamins. This vitamin (B9) is key to maintaining the healthy production of red blood cells and is especially important for women in the early stages of pregnancy or trying to conceive.

How to choose and store
♦ Choose an avocado that feels heavy for its size.
♦ Check it isn't bruised, damaged or squashed.
♦ Store at room temperature or in a cool place.

How to check for ripeness
♦ Hass avocado is green when unripe and blackens as it ripens; it should be dark brown, with a slightly purple hue when ripe.
♦ Don't use the color of the skin alone to determine ripeness—the feel is equally, if not more, important. Hold the avocado in the palm of your hand and gently squeeze; it should yield just a little. Never firmly press, squeeze or prod an avo as it bruises easily.

How to ripen a rock hard avocado
Avocado (along with bananas) releases ethylene gas, which is key to the ripening process. So place your unripe, hard avocado in a brown paper bag (or other container—an empty bread bin or cake tin works well). This will trap the ethylene gas and help it ripen more quickly. Store at room temperature.

Add a banana to the bag or tin, this will increase the amount of ethylene gas and speed up the process.

BLENDED

GREEN GAZPACHO SHOTS *DAIRY-FREE

On a scorching summer's day, a refreshing chilled soup can be soothing. This recipe takes its cue from Spanish gazpacho, but leans more toward vibrant Asian flavors. It looks stunning served in small shot glasses as an hors d'oeuvre. A summer party classic.

Serves 12 (¼ cup shots) as an hors d'oeuvre or 6 to 8 as an appetizer

1 garlic clove
½ cucumber (7 ounces)
½ green bell pepper, seeded and chopped
3 tablespoons blanched almonds
1 green chile, seeded
1 medium ripe avocado (about 5½ ounces flesh)
1 thick slice (about 2 ounces) stale country-style bread
A large handful of cilantro leaves
A large handful of basil leaves
3 scallions, white part only
3 tablespoons lime juice
1 cup chilled water
Sea salt and freshly ground black pepper

For the crab and mango salsa
½ cup ripe mango flesh, finely diced
½ cup freshly prepared white crab meat
½ green chile, seeded and finely chopped
1 tablespoon finely chopped cilantro leaves
Juice and zest of 1 lime
Ice cubes (optional)

1. In a food processor or blender, blend everything together (except the salsa) with a good pinch of sea salt and grind of black pepper until smooth. Add more water if needed to make a liquid consistency. Add more lime juice and seasoning to taste. Refrigerate for at least two hours or until very cold.

2. To serve, toss the diced mango with the crab, chile, chopped cilantro leaves, lime juice, and zest. Pour the soup into shot glasses, over ice if it's a warm day, and top with the crab and mango mixture. Serve immediately.

Before preparing, always rinse an unpeeled avocado under cold running water to remove any dirt, then dry thoroughly using a clean tea-towel or kitchen paper.

THAI CORN & COCONUT SOUP
*DAIRY-FREE

Full of fragrant Thai flavors, avocado enlivens this soup to make it a hearty, satisfying dish. Add shredded chicken to make it into a more substantial meal. Vegetarians can use vegetable stock and omit the Thai fish sauce, using a little soy sauce instead. It can also easily be made gluten-free; use gluten-free stock and use Tamari instead of fish sauce.

Serves 4

2 garlic cloves
2 red bird's eye chiles,
 seeded if less heat wanted
 (reserve a little for garnish)
4 kaffir lime leaves
3 to 4 large shallots
4 lemongrass stalks,
 coarsely chopped
A small bunch each of basil,
 and cilantro, leaves and
 stems chopped separately
1 × 13½ ounce can
 coconut milk
3½ cups chicken
 or vegetable stock
2 tablespoons Thai fish sauce
4 fresh corn cobs
2 limes, plus wedges to serve
1 medium ripe avocado,
 plus extra to serve
Sea salt and freshly
 ground black pepper

1. Place the garlic, chile, lime leaves, shallot, and lemongrass into a food processor, adding the basil and cilantro stems (about a tablespoon of each) and a splash of cold water before blending to a fine paste. Add to a large saucepan with another splash of water and cook, stirring, for 4 to 5 minutes until softened.

2. Add the coconut milk, stock, and fish sauce and bring to a boil. Reduce the heat and simmer for 20 minutes. Transfer to a liquidizer in batches, or use an immersion blender and blend until thick. Pass through a fine strainer, pressing the paste to extract as much flavor as possible.

3. Return the broth to the pan and bring back to a simmer. Cut the corn kernels away from the cobs and add them to the pan. Cook for about 10–12 minutes until tender.

4. Add the juice and zest of 1 lime and half of the basil and cilantro leaves. Blend half the soup in batches, with the avocado, until smooth. Return to the pan and stir to combine with the rest of the soup.

5. Add most of the remaining herbs (reserving a little for garnish), seasoning, and more lime juice to taste, then gently reheat.

6. Serve in bowls, scattered with some diced avocado, chopped chile, and remaining cilantro and basil leaves, torn. Add lime wedges on the side.

ROASTED GARLIC "AVIOLI" *VEGETARIAN *GLUTEN-FREE

A truly punchy aioli is sometimes the only thing you need for dunking roasted potatoes, fries, or a pile of crunchy vegetables. This version uses a gorgeous combination of avocado, Greek yogurt, and roasted garlic for a lovely mellow flavor.

Serves 4 to 6

For the avioli
6 garlic cloves, unpeeled
Juice and zest of ½ lemon
2 tablespoons Greek yogurt
1 small ripe avocado
Sea salt and freshly
    ground black pepper

To serve
A mixed selection of
    crudités e.g. radishes,
    baby carrots, cauliflower
    florets, celery

1. Preheat the oven to 350°F. Place the garlic cloves on a piece of foil, add 1 tablespoon of water and wrap up to make a package. Bake for 30 to 40 minutes until the garlic is soft. Carefully unwrap (beware of the hot steam) and let cool slightly. Squeeze the soft garlic from the skins into a food processor.

2. Add the lemon juice and zest, yogurt, and avocado flesh. Season generously and blend until smooth. Add more seasoning or lemon juice to taste.

3. Spoon into a bowl and place on a board or platter with piles of raw vegetables for dipping.

Cutting down on saturated fat or dodging dairy? Swap traditional butter for avocado "butter" by simply blending avocado with a squeeze of lime, a pinch of sea salt, and a pinch of cayenne or paprika. Delicious on toast or as a sandwich spread.

AVO "CAESAR" SALAD

A well-made Caesar salad is hard to beat on a summer's day—crisp salad leaves lightly coated in an ever-so-addictive creamy, tangy dressing. The classic recipe uses raw egg yolks and plenty of extra virgin olive oil to create creaminess, and cheats' versions often use store-bought mayonnaise. I've used avocado instead of these to make it super quick and easy, a little bit healthier, and even more addictive. Top with chicken, if you like.

Serves 4

For the avo Caesar dressing
1 small garlic clove,
    finely chopped
3 anchovies in oil,
    drained and chopped
1 heaping teaspoon
    Dijon mustard
4 tablespoons lemon juice
    (from 1–2 lemons)
¼ cup Parmesan, finely grated
½ large ripe avocado
Sea salt and freshly
    ground black pepper

For the salad
2 baby gem or Romaine
    lettuces, cut into thin
    wedges
10 marinated anchovy fillets
1 avocado, sliced
A large handful of homemade
    croutons (see tip)
Parmesan shavings

1. Start with the dressing: In a food processor, pulse the chopped garlic, anchovies, mustard, lemon juice, and Parmesan until smooth. Coarsely chop the avocado flesh and add to the food processor. Blend until smooth and add 2 to 3 tablespoons of chilled water if the dressing needs loosening—you want it to be a "drizzleable" consistency. Season to taste with salt, pepper, and a little more lemon juice.

2. For the salad, toss the lettuce leaves and anchovy fillets in a large bowl. Drizzle with just enough of the dressing to coat the leaves and toss together.

3. Divide between plates, add the sliced avocado, scatter with the homemade croutons, and finish with freshly shaved Parmesan.

To make croutons, toss torn cubes of stale white bread in a little oil and plenty of seasoning, bake in a preheated oven at 400°F for 5–10 minutes until golden and crisp.

TUNA SUSHI SALAD & WASABI AVOCADO

*DAIRY-FREE

Everything that's great about sushi in a salad. It's good for you, filling, fresh, and bursting with wonderful Japanese flavor. This punchy dressing has become something I make on a weekly basis! To make this gluten free use tamari instead of soy sauce. Vegetarians can serve this with pan-fried mushrooms or tofu instead of tuna.

Serves 2

For the avo wasabi dressing
½ small ripe avocado
½ teaspoon wasabi paste
3 tablespoons lime juice
1 teaspoon toasted sesame oil
2 teaspoons soy sauce
2 teaspoons yuzu (optional)
Sea salt and freshly ground
  black pepper

For the salad
¾ cup frozen edamame beans
1¼ cups cooked brown rice (or
  a mix of brown and wild rice)
¾ cup sugarsnap peas, sliced
1 tablespoon pickled ginger,
  drained and shredded
½ small ripe avocado, sliced
¾ cup radishes, finely sliced
4 scallions, finely sliced
1 tablespoon each black
  and white sesame seeds
9 ounces tuna steak
½ sheet of sushi nori, snipped
  into pieces (optional)

1. First make the dressing: Coarsely chop the avocado flesh and add to a small food processor with the remaining dressing ingredients. Pulse until smooth. Season to taste. Add 1 tablespoon of chilled water if the dressing needs loosening.

2. For the salad, cook the edamame beans in boiling, salted water for 2 minutes then drain and refresh under cold water. Add the beans to a large bowl along with the rice, sliced sugar snaps, pickled ginger, sliced avocado, radishes, and scallions. Add the dressing and gently toss together.

3. Spread the sesame seeds out on a plate. Preheat a frying pan until hot. Press the tuna into the seeds, turning to evenly coat both sides. Sear the tuna for 30 seconds to 1 minute on each side (depending on how thick it is—you want it to be rare). Transfer to a cutting board and thinly slice.

4. Divide the salad between two plates. Top with the sliced tuna. Sprinkle with any remaining seeds and nori pieces, if using.

SPIRALIZED SALAD & AVO SATAY DRESSING

*VEGETARIAN *DAIRY-FREE

When you're after something light yet satisfying, this satay style dressing breathes a little life into spiralized vegetables. To make this recipe gluten-free, swap the soy sauce for tamari.

Serves 4

For the dressing
1 tablespoon soy sauce
   (or tamari, to make this
   recipe gluten free)
1 heaping tablespoon freshly
   grated ginger
2 tablespoons coconut milk
3 tablespoons good-quality,
   crunchy peanut butter
½ teaspoon honey
¼ cup lime juice (about
   2 limes) and zest of 1 lime
½ large ripe avocado (about
   3½ ounces flesh), chopped
2 red chiles, seeded
   and finely chopped

For the spiralized salad
4 zucchini
2 large carrots
A small handful of
   cilantro leaves

1. Put the soy sauce, ginger, coconut milk, peanut butter, honey, and lime juice into a small food processor and blend to a paste.

2. Add the lime zest and avocado flesh. Process until smooth. Taste to check the seasoning and add a little more soy sauce and honey, if needed. Stir in most of the chile.

3. Spiralize the vegetables and transfer to a large bowl. Add the dressing and most of the cilantro leaves and toss together to coat. Divide between four plates, then finish with the remaining chile and cilantro. Serve immediately.

If you have leftover ripe avocado, you can use it for baking—try the Chewy Chocolate and Hazelnut Brownies on page 86 or the Banana and Walnut Bread on page 89.

AVOCADO "PESTO" WITH LINGUINE

This has to be one of my absolute favorite ways to use avocado. Its creamy texture works brilliantly as a substitute for olive oil in classic pesto and this spring twist combines savory pistachios with uplifting mint and nutty Parmesan, making a pile of linguine far too easy to demolish. To make this recipe vegetarian, use vegetarian hard cheese.

Serves 2

5½ ounces linguine
¾ cup frozen peas
1 zucchini, coarsely grated

For the avo "pesto"
½ cup pistachio kernels
½ garlic clove, finely chopped
1 medium ripe avocado
Juice of half a lemon, plus
   extra wedges to serve
½ cup Pecorino or Parmesan
   cheese, finely grated,
   plus extra to serve (or use
   vegetarian hard cheese)
⅓ cup mint leaves, plus
   extra to serve
Sea salt and freshly
   ground black pepper

1. Preheat the oven to 400°F. First make the pesto: Spread the pistachios out on a large baking sheet. Bake in the oven for 4 to 5 minutes until toasted. Let cool.

2. Add the cooled nuts to a food processor along with the garlic. Coarsely chop the avocado flesh. Add this to the food processor, along with the lemon juice, grated cheese, mint leaves, and 2 tablespoons cold water.

3. Add a good pinch of salt and pepper. Pulse to make a chunky, pesto consistency—add a little more water, if needed, or lemon juice to taste.

4. Next cook the pasta in boiling, salted water until al dente. Add the peas to the pan for the last minute of cooking time.

5. Drain well, reserving a couple of tablespoons of the cooking water and return to the pan. Add the grated zucchini and pesto, along with the reserved water to loosen. Toss together. Serve with grated cheese and mint leaves.

SWEET POTATO FRIES
& AVOCADO "MAYO"

*VEGETARIAN *DAIRY-FREE *GLUTEN-FREE

You may never return to regular mayonnaise again. This unintentionally dairy- and egg-free "mayo" is made simply from silky smooth avocados, fiery ginger, a teensy bit of garlic, and zippy limes, with an optional extra kick from chile. Slather it into a steak sandwich or dollop on the side of these addictive sweet potato fries.

Serves 4

For the sweet potato fries
4 sweet potatoes (about
   1¾ pounds)
3 tablespoons olive oil
3 tablespoons polenta
1 teaspoon paprika
Sea salt

For the "mayo"
1 large ripe avocado
1½ ounces ginger, peeled
   and finely grated
½ small garlic clove,
   crushed
Juice and zest of 1 lime
   (you need about
   3 tablespoons juice)
Dash of Tabasco (optional)
1 tablespoon olive oil

1. Preheat the oven to 400°F. Wash the sweet potatoes in cold water and dry thoroughly with a clean kitchen towel—there's no need to peel them. Then cut lengthwise into long ½-inch wide fries. Transfer to a large bowl. Add the oil and toss together to coat. Then add the polenta, paprika, and a good pinch of salt. Mix well to evenly coat.

2. Spread the fries between two large roasting pans. They need as much space as possible, so should be in a single layer. Bake for 35 to 40 minutes until tender and crisp.

3. Meanwhile, make the "mayo" dip. Place the avocado flesh in a food processor. Add the grated ginger, garlic, lime juice and zest, Tabasco (if using), olive oil, 1 tablespoon of cold water, and a large pinch of salt. Pulse until smooth. Transfer to a small dish and serve with the warm, crunchy sweet potato fries.

Smoothies provide a big whack of nutrients in one speedy hit. Avocados add a velvety smoothness and eliminate the need for dairy—while boosting the goodness levels even further. All of these smoothies are best made with chilled (or frozen) fruit.

SMOOTHIES

ALL *VEGETARIAN *GLUTEN-FREE *DAIRY-FREE

All serve 2

THE BERRY ONE

½ large ripe avocado
¾ cup frozen raspberries
(or use fresh)
½ ripe banana (about
2½ ounces)
2 teaspoons honey
¾ cup chilled coconut water

Hydrating, energizing, hunger-quashing, and utterly delicious, this smoothie is great any time of day, be it breakfast, post workout, or just when you need a pick-me-up.

Add the avocado flesh to a high-speed blender, food processor, or liquidizer along with the other ingredients. Blend until smooth. Pour into two glasses and serve immediately.

THE TROPICAL ONE

½ large ripe avocado
1 cup frozen or fresh
mango flesh
Juice of ½ lime
1 cup coconut milk
(the drinking kind, not
the canned variety)
½ to 1 teaspoon honey
(this will depend on the
sweetness of your mango)
2 passion fruit, seeds
and pulp scooped out
(optional)

Pretend you're basking in the sunshine on a beach with this smoothie and your day is bound to get off to a good start.

Add the avocado flesh to a high-speed blender, food processor, or liquidizer along with the remainder of the ingredients, except the passion fruit. Blend until smooth. Stir in the passion fruit pulp and seeds, if you like. Pour into two glasses and serve immediately.

THE NUTTY ONE

½ large ripe avocado
1 ripe banana, peeled
¾ cup chilled unsweetened
  almond milk
1 tablespoon almond
  (or peanut) butter
1 to 2 teaspoons honey,
  to taste, depending on
  the ripeness of your
  banana
1 tablespoon oats (check
  they are gluten-free)

This tastes much naughtier than it is, a little bit like a banana milkshake. Perfect for a speedy on-the-go breakfast or post workout, this smoothie will replenish those energy levels fast.

Add the avocado flesh to a high-speed blender, food processor, or liquidizer along with the remaining ingredients. Blend until smooth. Pour into two glasses and serve immediately.

THE GREEN ONE

½ large ripe avocado
¼ ripe banana
¾ cup spinach leaves
⅔ cup ripe melon
  (e.g. honeydew), cut
  into chunks
1 apple, quartered and
  core removed (about
  3½ ounces)
A thumb sized piece of
  ginger, peeled and grated
¾ cup chilled coconut water
10 mint leaves, to taste

This glorious green smoothie packs in the vitamins. Drink it for breakfast and feel all smug for the rest of the day.

Add the avocado flesh to a high-speed blender, food processor, or liquidizer along with the other ingredients. Blend until smooth. Pour into two glasses and serve immediately.

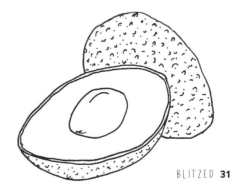

CLASSIC "GUAC" WITH TORTILLA CHIPS

*VEGETARIAN

This popular favorite will never go out of fashion, and the variations on this classic are endless. Some are incredibly basic, combining just avocado, lime, and salt, some use garlic instead of onion, or leave out tomatoes and cilantro. Others are mouth tinglingly spicy, and the texture ranges from rough and ready to super smooth. This is my favorite version, but it's worth experimenting to find yours.

Serves 4

For the tortilla chips
8 soft corn tortillas
2 tablespoons vegetable oil
1 teaspoon cumin seeds
1 teaspoon sea salt
1 teaspoon smoked paprika
Zest of 2 limes

For the guacamole
2 ripe avocados
1 red chile, seeded and finely chopped
½ cup cherry tomatoes, coarsely chopped
Juice and zest of 1 lime
1 tablespoon finely chopped red onion
A small handful of cilantro leaves, coarsely chopped

1. For the tortilla chips: Preheat the oven to 425°F. Lightly brush the tortillas with oil on both sides, then cut each tortilla into eight triangles.

2. Put the cumin seeds into a mortar and pestle with ½ teaspoon of sea salt and lightly crush. Mix in the smoked paprika. Put half of the tortilla triangles into a bowl and add half of the spice mix. Toss gently with clean hands to coat. Spread out in a single layer on a large baking sheet. Repeat with the rest of the tortillas. You will need at least three large baking sheets for this (or bake in batches).

3. Bake in the oven for about 5 minutes until crisp and golden. Let cool slightly.

4. Meanwhile, make the guacamole: Coarsely chop the avocado flesh, then transfer to a bowl along with the chopped chile and tomatoes, lime juice and zest, red onion, and cilantro. Add a good pinch of sea salt, smash together well, and check the seasoning. Serve immediately with the tortilla chips.

5. Mix the remaining ½ teaspoon of sea salt with the lime zest and sprinkle over the tortilla chips. Serve immediately with the guacamole.

GOOD-FOR-YOU "GUAC" WITH PITA CHIPS

*VEGETARIAN *DAIRY-FREE

As if guacamole needed any help on the health front. Yes, that's right, it's already good for you, but this version has added goodness from super nutritious kale, edamame, and pumpkin seeds to make it a really healthy snack. Warning: fennel and chile make pita chips dangerously addictive, so you may need to use some willpower. You can also make the pita chips with gluten-free pitas or serve with crudités.

Serves 4 to 6

For the fennel and chile pita chips
3 whole wheat pita breads
2 tablespoons olive oil
1½ teaspoon fennel seeds
½ teaspoon sea salt, plus extra for the guacamole
A large pinch dried red chile flakes

For the guacamole
⅔ cup frozen edamame beans
1 cup kale
1 small garlic clove, finely chopped
Juice and zest of 1 lemon
2 ripe avocados
1 tablespoon pumpkin seeds, toasted (optional)

1. First make the pita chips: Preheat the oven to 400°F. Cut the pitas in half horizontally to make two thin layers from each one. Cut each of these into rough triangles. Spread out on two large baking sheets and drizzle with the oil. Toss to coat. Crush the fennel seeds with the sea salt and chile flakes and sprinkle evenly over the pita triangles. Bake for about 8 minutes or until crisp.

2. For the guacamole, put the edamame and kale in a bowl and cover with boiling water. Set aside for 3 minutes, then drain and run under the cold tap. Drain thoroughly, then transfer to a food processor to coarsely chop, or do this by hand.

3. Put the garlic, lemon juice, and zest into a bowl. Coarsely chop the avocado flesh, mash with a fork, and then add this to the bowl along with the kale and edamame (or add this to the food processor and pulse briefly to combine). Add a generous pinch of salt, to taste, and mix well. Sprinkle with toasted pumpkin seeds before serving with the pita chips.

SMOKY AVOCADO, PEPPERS & CHORIZO

There's no going back once you've tried this—it might well become a regular weekend brunch fixture.

Serves 2

1 small garlic clove
1 large ripe avocado
A good squeeze of lemon juice
A large pinch of smoked
  paprika
1 roasted red bell pepper
  from a jar (about
  2½ ounces), drained
  and finely chopped
Sea salt and freshly
  ground black pepper
4½ ounces chorizo sausage,
  halved lengthwise
2 slices sourdough bread
A large handful of spinach
  or arugula leaves

1. Finely chop the garlic, then coarsely chop the avocado flesh and mix with the garlic. Add the lemon juice, smoked paprika, and chopped bell peppers. Lightly mash with a fork. Add salt and pepper and more lemon juice to taste.

2. Now heat a grill pan until hot and cook the chorizo for about 5 minutes, turning halfway until cooked through.

3. Toast the sourdough bread (either in the toaster or using the grill pan) and put onto individual plates. Spread each slice with a dollop of the smashed avocado, add a handful of leaves, and top with the chorizo. Serve immediately.

LEMONY AVO WITH ARUGULA & TROUT *DAIRY-FREE

Spread on toasted rye bread and topped with hot smoked trout, this gorgeously peppery Italian twist on a guacamole makes a delicious lunch. Top with a poached egg for a filling weekend brunch. For a vegetarian option, a creamy cheese works really well—add torn mozzarella or a spoonful of ricotta.

Serves 2

1 large ripe avocado
Sea salt
Juice of ½ lemon
2 teaspoons extra virgin olive oil or avocado oil
Black pepper
1¼ cups arugula leaves
2 large slices of rye or whole wheat bread
4½ ounces hot-smoked trout or salmon
Lemon wedges to serve

1. Coarsely mash the avocado flesh on a clean cutting board with a large pinch of sea salt and half of the lemon juice, then transfer to a bowl. Add 1 teaspoon of the olive oil or avocado oil and a generous grinding of black pepper. Mix well. Coarsely chop half of the arugula leaves and fold into the smashed avocado.

2. Toast the bread and arrange on two plates. Spoon the smashed avocado onto each slice of toast, then flake over the hot smoked fish. Toss the rest of the arugula leaves with the remaining olive oil and lemon juice and season. Serve alongside the toast with lemon wedges to squeeze over, if you like.

If your avocado is perfectly ripe in the morning and you plan to eat it later that evening, place it in the fridge to prevent it from overripening.

AVOCADO FATTOUSH
WITH FALAFEL *VEGETARIAN

Fattoush is a chopped salad with Lebanese roots that combines zingy spice sumac and fragrant herbs with the fresh crunch of summer vegetables—strips of toasted pita bread are added as a way of using them up. Smashing avocado with these flavors transforms this light salad into a sustaining and satisfying lunch. Make this dairy-free and vegan by leaving out the feta.

Serves 2

For the sumac spiced avocado
1 small garlic clove
Sea salt
1 tablespoon tahini paste
Juice of ½ lemon
1 large ripe avocado
A large pinch of sumac
⅓ cup cherry tomatoes, finely chopped
6 mint leaves, shredded, plus baby leaves to serve

To serve
2 flatbreads or pita breads, toasted or griddled
6 pre-made falafel
¼ cucumber, diced
⅓ cup cherry tomatoes, quartered
A handful of pitted Kalamata olives, halved
¼ red onion, finely sliced
⅓ cup feta cheese, crumbled (optional)

1. Crush the garlic in a mortar and pestle with a pinch of sea salt and twist of black pepper, then add to a bowl and stir in the tahini paste and lemon juice.

2. Scoop out the avocado flesh and coarsely chop. Add to the bowl with the sumac, chopped tomatoes, and shredded mint. Mix together until combined, and season to taste.

3. To serve, top a warm flatbread or pita with a spoonful of the avocado mixture and some falafel, then scatter with cucumber, tomatoes, olives, red onion, and crumbled feta, if using.

AVOCADO WITH PEAS, MINT & FETA
*VEGETARIAN

Avocado adds a luxurious note to this classic spring creation. These are easy-peasy hors d'oeuvres that are even easier to eat.

Serves 4 as an appetizer or 4 to 6 as hors d'oeuvres

1 cup frozen peas
2 scallions, white part only, finely chopped
1 ripe avocado, diced
1 heaping tablespoon finely chopped mint leaves, plus baby mint leaves to serve
1 tablespoon lemon juice (about ½ lemon)
1 teaspoon extra virgin olive oil or avocado oil, plus extra to drizzle (optional)
Sea salt and freshly ground black pepper
½ cup feta cheese
½ whole-grain or white baguette, sliced into 12 × ½-inch rounds

1. Preheat the broiler to medium. Add the peas to a pan of boiling water, bring back to a boil, simmer for 1 minute, drain, and refresh in a bowl of cold water. Drain again, then set aside 2 tablespoons of the peas. Blend the rest in a food processor with the scallions, half the avocado, chopped mint, lemon juice, and olive oil to make a rough puree. Transfer to a bowl.

2. Add the remaining avocado, mix to combine, then season to taste with salt and pepper. Add a little more lemon juice if you prefer a sharper taste.

3. Now toast the baguette rounds under the preheated broiler for about 1 minute, turning halfway. Once the crostini have cooled a little, spoon some of the smashed mixture onto each one. Transfer to a plate or serving platter, crumble over the feta, and top with mint leaves. Drizzle with extra virgin olive oil or avocado oil, if you like.

AVOCADO HUMMUS & ROASTED DUKKAH

Who doesn't love hummus? It's a great go-to savory snack when you need to surrender to those sudden hunger pangs and an instant, healthy energy boost. Avocado enriches this hummus and the hit of flavor from this easy Egyptian spice mix really livens it up. . You can also sprinkle this versatile spice mix over pita chips or toss with vegetables before roasting.

Serves 4 to 6

For the roasted dukkah

1 tablespoon each blanched
   almonds and hazelnuts
2 teaspoons sesame seeds
1 teaspoon cumin seeds
½ teaspoon coriander seeds
½ teaspoon fennel seeds

For the hummus

1 garlic clove, finely chopped
1 tablespoon tahini paste
2 tablespoons lemon juice
   and zest of ½ lemon
Sea salt
1 (14-ounce) can chickpeas,
   drained
1 ripe avocado
2 tablespoons chopped
   cilantro, plus a small handful
   of leaves to garnish

To serve

Warm flatbreads, cut
   into strips

1. Preheat the oven to 350°F. First prepare the roasted dukkah: Spread the nuts out in a large roasting pan. Bake for 5 minutes, then scatter over the remaining seeds and spices. Roast for another 2 to 3 minutes until fragrant. Keep an eye on them as you don't want the spices to burn. Set aside to cool slightly, then transfer to a mortar and pestle and lightly crush or coarsely grind in a food processor.

2. Now make the hummus: Put the garlic in a food processor with the tahini paste, lemon zest and juice, and a large pinch of salt. Set aside a tablespoon of chickpeas and add the remainder to the food processor along with 2 tablespoons of

the spice mix and the avocado. Process to a chunky puree (you want to keep some of the texture).

3. Add the chopped cilantro, mix well, and season to taste.

4. Spoon into a serving dish, top with the reserved chickpeas, and sprinkle with a little more of the dukkah spices. Serve with warmed flatbreads to dip.

CHOPPED

AVO SHRIMP COCKTAIL & CHARRED LETTUCE

*DAIRY-FREE

A timeless classic, this avocado twist on the retro appetizer brings this favorite dish up to date.

Serves 2

1 baby gem lettuce, cut in
  half lengthwise
Olive oil for brushing
7 ounces cooked shrimp
1 ripe avocado, diced
Cayenne pepper

For the Marie Rose sauce
½ cup good quality
  mayonnaise
1 tablespoon ketchup
¼ teaspoon Tabasco sauce
Juice of ½ lemon, plus extra,
  and lemon wedges to serve
⅓ teaspoon Worcestershire
  sauce
Sea salt and freshly
  ground black pepper
1 tablespoon chopped chives

1. First make the Marie Rose sauce: In a bowl combine the mayonnaise, ketchup, Tabasco, lemon juice, and Worcestershire sauce. Season to taste with a little sea salt and freshly ground pepper. Add a little more lemon juice if needed, then stir in half of the chopped chives

2. Preheat a ridged grill pan until very hot. Lightly brush the cut side of each lettuce half with a little oil and season. When the grill pan is very hot, add the lettuce halves cut side down for 2 minutes until lines appear. Turn over and cook for a minute, then transfer one lettuce half, cut side up, to each plate.

3. Add the shrimp to the Marie Rose sauce and mix well. Toss the diced avocado with a squeeze of lemon juice and remaining chives. Top each lettuce half with some of the shrimp cocktail, then spoon over the avocado. Sprinkle with a little cayenne pepper. Serve with lemon wedges on the side to squeeze over.

For those with good knife skills and more experienced cooks, you can use a knife to remove the pit. Hold the avocado in place and in one swift motion firmly lodge the length of a heavy, sharp knife into the surface of the pit—it should stay lodged there. Then hold the avocado and gently twist the knife to release the pit. Be careful here as avocado flesh is slippery.

AVO SALMON CEVICHE WITH TOSTADAS

*DAIRY-FREE

The perfect light bite for a balmy summer evening—zesty lime, fragrant cilantro, and a little kick from chile make these dangerously addictive. Make sure your salmon is a fresh as possible.

Serves 2 to 3
Makes 6 mini tostadas

7 ounces very fresh salmon, skinless and boneless
½ teaspoon sea salt
½ cup lime juice (about 2 to 3 limes)
1 red chile, seeded and finely chopped
¼ small red onion, finely chopped
6 mini corn tortillas or 4 standard sized corn tortillas
Vegetable oil, for frying
Paprika, to sprinkle
1 ripe avocado
2 tablespoons chopped cilantro

1. Cut the salmon into ½-inch cubes as evenly as you can. Transfer to a bowl, then add the salt, lime juice, chile, and red onion. Mix well and refrigerate for 10 minutes.

2. Meanwhile, make the tostadas: If you can find mini corn tortillas, use these. If not, buy the standard corn tortillas and use a 4-inch circular cutter to cut out six smaller rounds. Use the trimmings to make tortilla chips. Pour enough oil into a frying pan to cover the base in a thin layer and heat until very hot. Carefully fry the tortillas in batches, for about 30 seconds on each side, and transfer to a plate lined with paper towels. Sprinkle with sea salt and a little paprika.

3. Dice the avocado flesh into ½-inch cubes and transfer to a bowl. Strain the marinated salmon mixture of any excess lime juice and add to the bowl with the avocado, then add the cilantro and gently toss together. Taste to check the seasoning.

4. Top each tostada with a spoonful of ceviche and eat immediately.

CORN FRITTERS & CHILE-AVO SALSA

This sprightly salsa will perk up even the dreariest of winter mornings. Pile it onto these mouth-watering corn fritters— with a runny fried egg, if you like.

Serves 2 to 3 (makes 6 fritters)

For the salsa

1 ripe avocado
Juice and zest of 1 lime
1 cup cherry tomatoes, quartered
1 red chile, seeded and finely chopped
2 scallions, finely sliced
2 tablespoons chopped cilantro leaves
Sea salt

For the fritters

1 (12-ounce) can corn, drained
1 large egg, beaten
3 tablespoons self-rising flour
2 tablespoons finely chopped chives
½ cup feta cheese or hard goats cheese, cubed
Butter and vegetable oil for frying

To serve
Fried eggs (optional)

1. For the salsa, dice the avocado flesh and put in a large bowl. Add the lime juice and zest, mix well, then add the tomatoes, most of the chile, scallions, chopped cilantro, and a pinch of sea salt. Set aside.

2. Now make the fritters: Put half the corn, egg, flour, and a large pinch of salt into a food processor. Pulse until smooth, then transfer to a bowl. Fold in the rest of the corn, chives, and feta

3. Heat the butter and vegetable oil in a large, nonstick frying pan. When hot, add spoonfuls of the mixture. You'll need about 3 tablespoons per fritter. Cook, in batches, over medium heat for 2 to 3 minutes on each side until golden. You can keep them warm in a low oven while you cook the rest.

4. Stack two or three fritters onto each plate, add a spoonful of salsa, and top with the fried egg. Sprinkle with the reserved chile. Top with a fried egg, if you like.

BOILED EGGS & CRISPY AVOCADO "FRIES"

These melt-in-the-mouth avocado fries bring a whole new dimension to boiled eggs. Crispy on the outside and beautifully buttery in the center, they are just perfect for dipping into a hot, runny yolk. Use vegetarian hard cheese to make this vegetarian.

Serves 2

1 firm but ripe avocado
¼ cup all-purpose flour
¼ teaspoon paprika or
    cayenne pepper
½ teaspoon fine salt
3 eggs
½ cup Japanese-style
    panko bread crumbs
¼ cup finely grated
    Parmesan cheese, or
    vegetarian hard cheese
Vegetable oil, for frying

1. Take three plates and place them next to each other. Put the flour, paprika or cayenne pepper, and salt onto the first plate. Crack one egg onto the second plate and lightly whisk, then put the bread crumbs, Parmesan, and some seasoning onto the final plate and mix well.

2. Take a slice of avocado and gently toss in the flour to coat, then dip in the beaten egg and finally turn in the bread crumb mixture until evenly coated. Repeat with the remaining slices.

3. Pour enough oil into a nonstick frying pan to cover the base. Set over medium heat for a few minutes. When hot, add the crumbed avocado slices in batches and cook for 1 to 2 minutes each side until crisp and golden. Transfer to a plate lined with paper towels. If you're not sure if the oil is hot enough, test with a small piece of bread. The bread should sizzle on touching the oil and turn golden after a minute or so.

4. When the avocado is almost done, put the remaining eggs into a pan of cold water. Bring to a boil, then set the timer and simmer for 3 minutes. Remove immediately and place in egg cups or small ramekins. Use a knife to slice off the top of each egg. Serve a few crispy avocado slices with the soft-boiled eggs to dip in.

To cook the crumbed avocado fries with less fat, you can bake them on a baking sheet lined with parchment paper in a preheated oven (425°F) for 10 minutes.

CRISPBREAD, MACKEREL & DILL-PICKLED AVO

These homemade crispbreads are simple to make, but if you're short on time, there are store-bought versions. Alternatively, this would also work as a topping for toasted rye bread or a whole wheat bagel. The crispbreads will keep for a few days in an airtight container.

Serves 4
Makes 8 to 10 crispbreads

For the seeded crispbreads
¾ cup rye flour
¾ cup all-purpose flour
¾ cup whole wheat flour
1 teaspoon fine salt
½ cup mixed seeds (e.g. sunflower, pumpkin, sesame, flaxseed)
1 teaspoon caraway seeds
2 teaspoons honey
¼ cup olive oil
½ cup water

For the avo and cucumber pickle
½ cucumber
½ teaspoon fine salt
2 tablespoons white wine vinegar
2 tablespoons lemon juice (plus the zest of 1 lemon)
1 tablespoon superfine sugar
2 tablespoons chopped dill, plus a few sprigs to garnish
1 firm but ripe avocado, sliced

cream cheese, to serve
9 ounces smoked peppered mackerel, to serve

1. For the crispbreads, preheat the oven to 350°F. Mix together the flours, salt, and ½ cup of mixed seeds in a large bowl and add half of the caraway seeds. Whisk the honey and olive oil with the water. Make a well in the center of the dry ingredients and pour in most of the liquid. Mix together to make a dough, adding the remainder of the liquid if necessary to bring the dough together.

2. Knead briefly, then roll out the dough on a lightly floured surface to a large rectangle ⅛-inch thick. Sprinkle with the remaining seeds and lightly roll into the surface of the dough. Cut the dough into 6 to 8 rectangles. Transfer to two large baking sheets lined with parchment paper. Gather up the dough trimmings and reroll to get a few extra. Bake for about 20 minutes until pale golden, then transfer to a cooling rack.

3. For the pickle, halve the cucumber lengthwise, scrape out the seeds, then finely slice into half moons and place in a colander in the sink. Toss with the salt. Place a piece of parchment paper on top of the cucumber and put something heavy—a can works. Set aside for 15 minutes.

4. Meanwhile, put the vinegar, lemon juice, and sugar in a small bowl and stir until the sugar dissolves. Then add half of the dill.

5. Rinse the cucumber of salt and dry between paper towels. Add to the pickling liquid along with the avocado. Cover and refrigerate for 1 hour, then strain, discarding the liquid, and toss with the remaining dill. Season to taste.

6. Spread a little cream cheese onto a crispbread, top with the pickled avocado and cucumber, and finish with flaked smoked mackerel. Add a few sprigs of dill.

AVO TUNA TARTARE & SESAME TOASTS *DAIRY-FREE

This savory soy sauce, sesame, and ginger dressing goes so well with meaty tuna, and is balanced with the cooling crunch of cucumber and mellow avocado. A delicious topping for mouth-watering sesame toasts.

Serves 4 as an appetizer

1 large ripe but firm avocado, diced into ¾-inch cubes
½ cucumber, seeded and chopped into ¾-inch cubes
10 ounces fresh tuna steak, diced into ½-inch cubes
2 scallions, finely sliced
1 teaspoon sesame seeds, toasted

For the sesame toasts
1 thin white baguette (cut into 12 × ½-inch slices)
1 tablespoon toasted sesame oil
4 teaspoons each white and black sesame seeds

For the dressing
1 tablespoon soy sauce
Juice of 2 limes, plus lime wedges to serve
1 teaspoon toasted sesame oil
½–1 red chile
1 tablespoon ginger, finely grated
1 tablespoon chopped cilantro, plus a handful of leaves

1. First make the dressing: Put the soy sauce, lime juice, sesame oil, chile to taste, ginger, and chopped cilantro into a food processor. Pulse until smooth, then transfer to a bowl.

2. Now start the tartare: Place the diced avocado and cucumber into another bowl, add half the dressing, and mix gently to combine.

3. Preheat the broiler to high, ready for the sesame toasts. To make, spread the baguette slices out in a single layer on a baking sheet. Broil until just toasted then remove from the broiler, turn over, and brush the untoasted side with the sesame oil. Spread the mixed sesame seeds evenly on top of the toasts then return to the broiler for 30 to 60 seconds until toasted and golden.

4. Add the diced tuna and reserved cilantro leaves to the bowl with the remaining dressing and toss together.

5. To serve, spoon a quarter of the avocado and cucumber mixture into an 3-inch chef's ring (or use a biscuit cutter) on the center of a plate and spread out evenly to fill the ring. Spoon the tuna tartare on top. Garnish with a little scallion and a sprinkling of toasted sesame seeds. Repeat with the remaining three servings on individual plates. Serve with the sesame toasts on the side.

If you don't have a chef's ring, you can also serve the tartare in small glasses.

SHRIMP & AVOCADO SPRING ROLLS

Clean, fresh, and fragrant—velvety smooth avocado and succulent, sweet shrimp are a wonderful double act in this twist on this Vietnamese classic (photo overleaf).

Serves 4

3 ounces rice noodles
8 rice paper wrappers
16 cooked large shrimp
   (about 5½ ounces), peeled
   and halved horizontally
A small handful of
   cilantro leaves
2 to 3 tablespoons finely
   shredded mint leaves
⅓ cucumber, seeded and
   sliced into thin lengths
1 carrot, cut into matchsticks
   or coarsely grated
¼ iceberg lettuce,
   finely shredded
1 large ripe avocado,
   thinly sliced
3 tablespoons salted peanuts,
   coarsely chopped

For the dipping sauce
Juice and zest of 2 limes
2 teaspoons light brown
   or palm sugar
2 tablespoons Thai fish sauce
1 tablespoon soy sauce
1 bird's eye chile, seeded
   and finely chopped

1. Put the rice noodles in a bowl and cover with boiling water. Leave for 4 to 5 minutes, drain well, and run under cold water. Set aside.

2. Fill a bowl with cold water. Briefly dip a rice paper wrapper into the water, shake off any excess, and transfer to a clean cutting board. This should make them pliable. Be careful not to submerge for too long, as they may become delicate and tricky to handle.

3. Place four shrimp halves in a line in the center of a rice paper wrapper, then add a line of cilantro and mint alongside. Top with a few rice noodles, a little cucumber, carrot, lettuce, and avocado.

4. Add a sprinkle of peanuts, then fold the bottom of the wrapper over the filling. Fold in the sides and roll up. Repeat with the remaining wrappers and filling.

5. For the dipping sauce, whisk the lime juice and zest with the sugar, fish sauce, and soy sauce. Stir in the chile and add water to taste.

6. Serve the spring rolls with the dipping sauce and a sprinkling of cilantro leaves.

SWEET POTATO HASH
& SMOKY FRIJOLES
*VEGETARIAN

Comforting sweet potato hash, smoky black beans, and charred, buttery avocado make this a warming veggie supper. This can easily be made gluten-free—just use gluten-free vegetable stock.

Serves 4

2 pounds sweet potato
 (about 4), cut into
 1¼-inch chunks
¾ cup feta cheese
Lime wedges
4 eggs, for frying

For the frijoles
2 teaspoons cumin seeds
1 tablespoon olive oil
1 red onion, finely chopped
2 garlic cloves, finely chopped
1 teaspoon dried oregano
1 teaspoon smoked paprika
1 (14-ounce) black beans,
 drained
1 cup hot vegetable stock
Sea salt and freshly
 ground black pepper

For the hash
¼ teaspoon dried red chile
 flakes or 1 red chile, chopped
1 garlic clove, crushed
4 scallions, finely sliced
1½ cups cilantro, stems and
 leaves chopped separately
1–2 tablespoons oil
2 firm but ripe avocados

1. Place the sweet potatoes in a microwave-proof bowl. Cover and microwave at 600W for 10 minutes or until completely tender (alternatively, steam or roast, covered, in the oven).

2. To make the frijoles: Preheat a deep sauté or frying pan, add the cumin seeds, and cook for about a minute until toasted and fragrant. Add the oil, onion, and garlic and soften gently for 10 minutes. Add the oregano, smoked paprika, black beans, and stock and slowly bring to a simmer. Cook gently for 15 minutes, stirring occasionally, then season to taste.

3. Coarsely mash the sweet potatoes with a fork, then mix in the red chile flakes or fresh chile, crushed garlic, scallions, chopped cilantro stems, and some seasoning. Heat a splash of oil in a large frying pan. Roughly divide the sweet potato mash

into four equal amounts. Add each spoonful to the pan and cook for 3 to 4 minutes until crispy and golden, flip over, and cook for another 2 to 3 minutes. Remove from the pan and keep warm. Return the pan to the heat, add a little more oil, and fry the eggs.

4. Meanwhile, heat a ridged grill pan until hot. Lightly brush the cut side of each avocado half with a little oil and season. When the pan is hot, place the halves cut-side down and cook for 1 to 2 minutes over high heat until grill marks appear.

5. To serve, place a sweet potato hash on each plate, spoon over the frijoles and top with a fried egg. Serve each with a grilled avocado half. Crumble over the feta and sprinkle with chopped cilantro leaves and chile. Serve with lime wedges on the side.

PAN-FRIED MACKEREL, AVO & GRAPEFRUIT

*GLUTEN-FREE *DAIRY-FREE

Bittersweet grapefruit contrasts so well with rich avocado and juicy, succulent mackerel. This is an effortless appetizer that's really easy to make but bound to knock the socks off your guests.

Serves 4 as an appetizer or light lunch

2 pink grapefruit (reserve 2 tablespoons juice for the dressing)
1 fennel bulb, trimmed
1 ripe avocado, sliced
1½ cups watercress
4 fresh mackerel fillets
Peanut oil

For the dressing

2 tablespoons extra virgin olive oil, plus a little extra for the mackerel
1 tablespoon lemon juice or white wine vinegar
1 teaspoon Dijon mustard
1 teaspoon honey
Sea salt and freshly ground black pepper
½ red onion, finely sliced
1 red chile, seeded and finely chopped

1. Start by removing the pith and peel from the grapefruit with a serrated knife. Then cut in between the pith to release the segments and transfer to a large bowl.

2. Now make the dressing: Squeeze the grapefruit juice from the remaining pithy membranes into a bowl (you only need 2 tablespoons of juice). Add the olive oil, lemon juice or vinegar, mustard, and honey to the bowl, whisk together, and season to taste. Add the red onion and chile.

3. Slice the fennel as thinly as you can, then add to the bowl with the grapefruit segments, along with the avocado slices and watercress.

4. Heat a dry frying pan until hot. Lightly rub the fish fillets with a little oil on both sides, then season all over. Add to the hot pan skin-side down. Cook for 3 minutes over medium–high heat until the skin turns crisp, then flip over and cook for another minute or until just cooked through. Remove the pan from the heat.

5. Pour the dressing over the salad and gently toss together to coat. Divide the salad between four plates and top each one with a mackerel fillet.

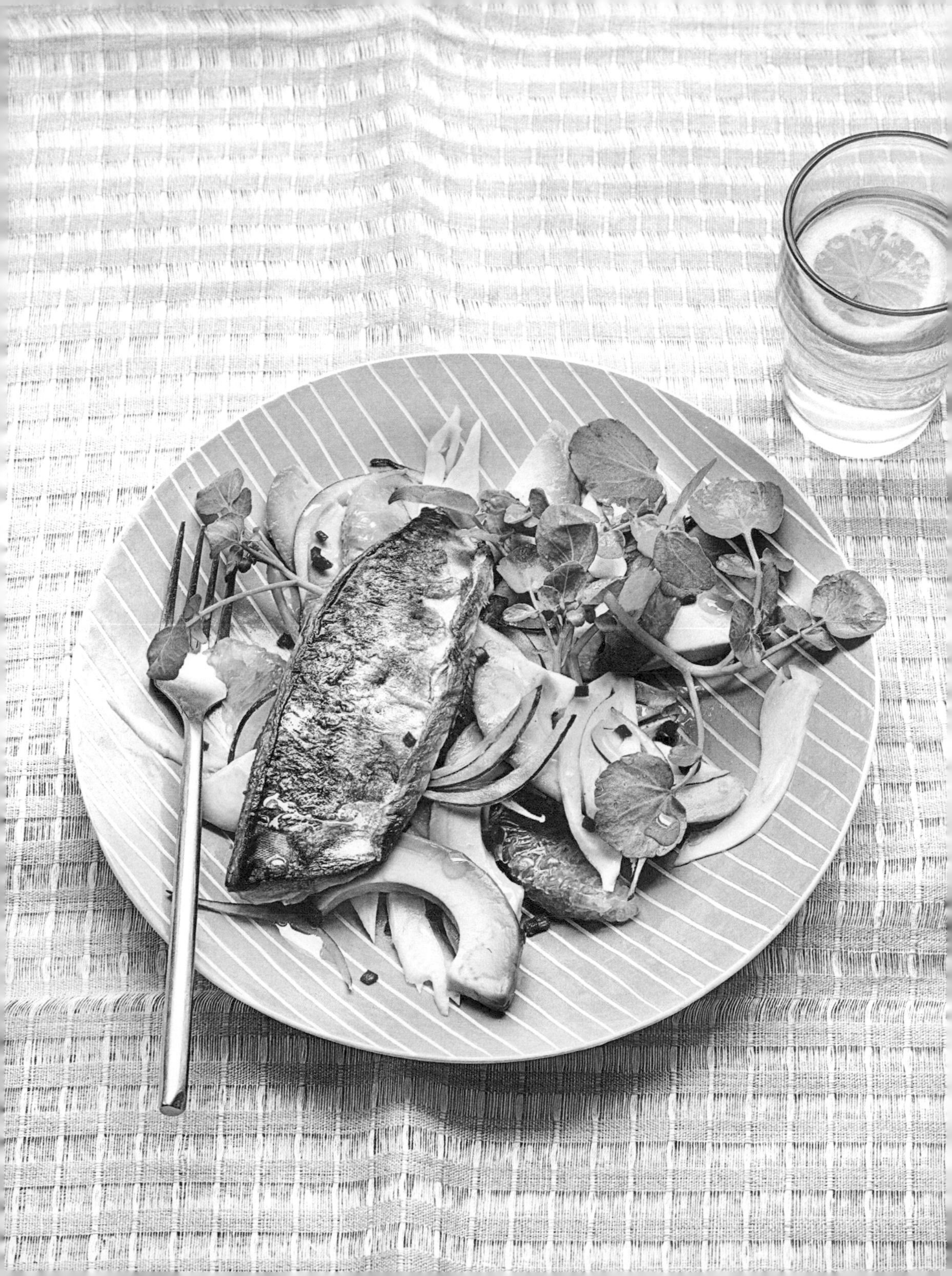

STEAK, CHIMICHURRI & CORN SALSA

*GLUTEN-FREE *DAIRY-FREE

Argentinian chimichurri sauce is big, bold, and packs a world of flavor into one hit. Use this as a dressing for a tomato-avo-corn salsa and you've got the perfect adornment for juicy, rare steak. This is delicious on its own, but you can also serve with sweet potato chips or a green salad alongside.

Serves 4

For the salsa
½ red onion, finely chopped
1 garlic clove, finely chopped
1 red chile, seeded and
   finely chopped
2 tablespoons red wine
   vinegar
4 teaspoons olive oil
¼ teaspoon hot chile powder
Sea salt and freshly
   ground black pepper
1 corn cob
1 tablespoon finely
   chopped parsley
½ teaspoon dried oregano
1 avocado, pit removed,
   peeled, and diced
1 cup cherry tomatoes,
   quartered

For the steak
4 ribeye or sirloin steaks
2 teaspoons olive oil

1. First make the chimichurri salsa: Put the onion, garlic, chile, and vinegar in a bowl and set aside.

2. Meanwhile, heat a grill pan or frying pan until hot. Mix 1 teaspoon of the olive oil with the chile powder and some seasoning. Rub the corn cob all over with the spiced oil. When hot, add the corn to the grill pan and cook for 10 to 15 minutes, turning every couple of minutes until lightly charred and cooked through. Transfer to a cutting board and let cool for a few minutes.

3. Return the pan to the heat. Brush each steak all over with ½ teaspoon of oil and season. When hot, add the steaks and cook over high heat for 3 minutes, turn over, and cook for another 2 to 3 minutes. This should be medium rare, but will depend on the thickness of your steaks. Cook for longer if you prefer them less pink. Transfer to a warm plate and set aside to rest for a few minutes. You may need to cook the steak in batches depending on the size of your pan.

4. Add the parsley, oregano, and remaining oil to the bowl with the salsa. On a clean cutting board, firmly hold the cooled corn cob on its end and use a sharp knife to cut away the charred kernels. Add these to the salsa, along with the diced avocado flesh and cherry tomatoes. Toss together and season to taste.

5. Serve the steaks with the chimichurri salsa.

AVOCADO & BACON "NIÇOISE"

*GLUTEN-FREE *DAIRY-FREE

As a rule, a Niçoise salad is not to be messed with—perfectly balanced as all French dishes tend to be. But swap tuna for crisp, smoked bacon and add in soft and creamy sliced avocado, and you have a twist on this classic that deserves to be eaten.

Serves 4

1¼ pounds new potatoes
7 ounces green beans, trimmed
8–12 slices thick bacon
4 large eggs, at room temperature
2 little gem lettuces, separated into leaves
1½ cups mini plum or cherry tomatoes, quartered lengthwise
2 avocados, sliced
16 black olives, pitted and halved

For the dressing
2 teaspoons Dijon or whole-grain mustard
2 teaspoons honey
¼ cup olive oil
2 tablespoons white wine vinegar
Sea salt and freshly ground black pepper

1. Preheat the broiler to high. Cook the potatoes in a large pan of boiling salted water for about 20 minutes until tender. Add the green beans for the last 4 minutes of the cooking time then drain and run under cool water until cold.

2. Meanwhile, cook the bacon for about 5 minutes, turning halfway until crisp. Set aside.

3. Put the eggs into a small saucepan and cover with cold water. Bring to a boil, then set a timer and simmer for 3 minutes for a runny yolk, 4 minutes for soft set yolk up to 5 minutes if you prefer a harder set yolk. Drain, put the eggs in a bowl, and cover with cold water. Then peel and cut the eggs in half.

4. Next make the dressing by whisking all the ingredients together with a pinch of salt and generous grind of black pepper.

5. Slice the cooled potatoes and add to a large salad bowl with the green beans, lettuce leaves, tomatoes, sliced avocado, and olives. Drizzle over the dressing and gently toss the salad. Divide between four plates then top with the halved eggs and crispy bacon. Serve immediately.

Very fresh eggs are difficult to peel. Use eggs that are a couple of weeks old to make removing the shell easier.

"BLAT" (BACON, LETTUCE, AVOCADO & TOMATO)

*DAIRY-FREE

Avocado gives the ultimate upgrade to this breakfast or brunch classic. Pile it high, and if you're feeling extra hungry, add a fried egg on top to really finish it off.

Serves 2

6 slices thick bacon
1 firm but ripe avocado
1 tablespoons good-quality
   mayonnaise (optional)
½ lemon
Sea salt and freshly
   ground black pepper
4 thick slices of your
   favorite bread (soft white
   farmhouse loaf works well)
4 crispy lettuce leaves
1 large vine ripened
   tomato, sliced
Ketchup (optional),
   to serve

1. Preheat the broiler to high. Cook the bacon for about 5 minutes, turning halfway until the fat is golden and starting to crisp.

2. Mash half the avocado flesh with the mayonnaise, if using, and a good squeeze of lemon. Add salt and freshly ground black pepper to taste. Set aside.

3. Heat a ridged, nonstick grill pan until hot. Thickly slice the remaining avocado half. Grill the slices for 30 seconds on each side, or until grill marks appear.

4. Toast the bread, spread with the avocado "mayo," then layer with the lettuce, tomato, grilled avocado, and bacon. Sandwich together with the remaining slices of toasted bread. Serve immediately, with ketchup, if you like.

When chopping avocado, some people prefer to leave the skin on to give them more grip. While holding a pitted avocado half in place, cut side up, carefully dice the avocado flesh or slice without cutting through to the skin. Then scoop out the flesh with a spoon to keep the pieces intact.

GREEN GREATNESS
SALAD *VEGETARIAN *GLUTEN-FREE *DAIRY-FREE

Eat this on its own as a virtuous, feel-good lunch, or crumble over feta and add chicken, mackerel, salmon, or eggs for a more filling meal.

Serves 4

1 cup quinoa (or about
  2¾ cups cooked)
2 cups purple sprouting
  broccoli or broccolini,
  cut into pieces
1¼ cups frozen edamame
  beans
2 tablespoons whole
  almonds, skin on
2 tablespoons mixed seeds
  (sunflower and pumpkin
  seeds work well)
3½ ounces spinach
2 ripe avocados, sliced
4 scallions, finely sliced
A small handful each of
  parsley and mint leaves,
  coarsely chopped

For the dressing
3 tablespoons extra
  virgin olive oil
¼ cup lemon juice (1 lemon)
2 teaspoons honey
1 garlic clove, squashed
Sea salt and freshly ground
  black pepper

1. Cook the quinoa in a large pan of boiling water or gluten-free vegetable stock for 15 to 20 minutes, or until tender. Drain well and transfer to a large bowl.

2. Meanwhile, cook the broccoli in a pan of boiling water for 3 to 4 minutes until just tender, adding the edamame for the last minute of cooking time. Drain well, then add to a bowl of cold or iced water to prevent the vegetables from overcooking.

3. For the dressing, place the oil, lemon juice, honey, and garlic in a clean mason jar with a pinch of salt and pepper. Secure the lid and shake well until the dressing has emulsified. Set aside.

4. Heat a dry frying pan until hot, add the almonds, and cook for a couple of minutes, tossing the pan occasionally until toasted. Set aside to cool slightly, then chop. Return the pan to the heat, add the seeds, and toast for a couple of minutes. Set aside.

5. Remove the garlic clove from the dressing, then pour over the quinoa. Add the cooked and cooled vegetables, spinach, sliced avocado, scallions, and herbs. Gently toss together to dress the salad. Scatter with the toasted seeds and nuts.

GREEN & CLEAN
POTATO SALAD

*VEGETARIAN *GLUTEN-FREE

This is an addictive alternative to the traditional potato salad. It is delicious in its own right, but being free from mayonnaise, this is the perfect choice for those who can't eat eggs or simply prefer a more nourishing, cleaner alternative. Serve on a sunny summer's day with roast chicken and a peppery watercress or green salad.

Serves 4

1¼ pounds new potatoes
1 ripe avocado
1 teaspoon Dijon mustard
1 tablespoon lemon juice
2 tablespoons Greek yogurt
½ teaspoon honey
Sea salt and freshly
  ground black pepper
½ red onion or 4 spring
  onions, finely chopped
A small handful of
  flat-leaf parsley,
  chopped

1. Cook the potatoes in a large pan of boiling, salted water for about 20 minutes until tender. Drain well, cool under cold running water, and set aside.

2. Meanwhile, coarsely chop half the avocado flesh and place in a food processor along with the mustard, lemon juice, yogurt, honey, and a generous pinch of salt and pepper. Pulse until smooth and season to taste.

3. Halve or quarter any large potatoes, then add to a bowl. Cut the remaining avocado into chunky cubes and add to the bowl, along with the red (or spring) onion and parsley. Add the dressing and toss gently to coat. Serve immediately.

AVOCADO SALSA VERDE
*DAIRY-FREE

Rich nuggets of silky smooth avocado soften the salty, sour, herby punch of a traditional salsa verde in this version. It tastes delicious with barbecued lamb cutlets or roasted white fish.

Serves 4

1 garlic clove, finely chopped
1 tablespoon white wine vinegar
1 teaspoon Dijon mustard
Freshly ground black pepper
Pinch of sugar or ½ teaspoon honey
1 tablespoon capers in brine, drained and coarsely chopped
¼ cup cornichons, drained and sliced
2 anchovies in oil, drained, finely chopped (optional)
1 heaping tablespoon shallot, finely chopped (about 1 shallot)
½ cup each flat-leaf parsley and mint leaves, coarsely chopped
3 tablespoons extra virgin olive oil or avocado oil
1 large ripe avocado, cut into ½-inch dice
Freshly grilled lamb or chicken cutlets, or fish, to serve

1. Place the garlic in a medium-sized bowl. Add the vinegar, mustard, some freshly ground black pepper, and a pinch of sugar or a little honey. Whisk with a fork to combine.

2. Add the capers, cornichons, and anchovies, if using, to the same bowl. Stir in the chopped shallot, chopped herbs, and olive or avocado oil and mix gently to combine.

3. Mash ¼ of the avocado cubes with a fork until smooth. Stir this into the salsa, then gently mix with the remaining avocado. Serve with freshly grilled lamb or chicken cutlets, or fish.

Toss prepared avocado flesh with a little lemon or lime juice to prevent discoloration.

NUTTY CHOC-AVO
SPREAD *VEGETARIAN *DAIRY-FREE *GLUTEN-FREE

Store-bought chocolate spreads are high in energy but low in nutrients. Avocado boosts the nourishing power of this homemade breakfast spread and it's also free from any nasty additives and preservatives. Make a batch for the weekend and slather onto your favorite toast. You could also try swapping hazelnuts for almonds or cashews. It will keep chilled, in an airtight container, for up to four days.

Makes 1 × 10-ounce jar

¾ cup blanched hazelnuts
1 ripe avocado
½ tsp vanilla extract
⅓ cup good-quality cocoa
  powder (I use Green &
  Blacks; check the label
  to ensure it is dairy-free),
  sifted
¼ cup maple syrup
Sea salt
Toast, to serve

1. Preheat the oven to 350°F. Spread the nuts out on a baking sheet and cook for 10 minutes until toasted and turning golden. Let cool.

2. Transfer the cooled nuts to a food processor and pulse until finely ground. Continue to pulse until they turn to a paste.

3. Coarsely chop the avocado flesh and add to the food processor along with the vanilla extract, cocoa, maple syrup, and a pinch of sea salt. Process until smooth.

4. Transfer to a jar or airtight container and keep chilled. Spread over freshly toasted bread.

MAPLE PECAN
CHOCOLATE PUDDING
*VEGETARIAN *DAIRY-FREE *GLUTEN-FREE

These delightfully addictive make-ahead desserts feel as indulgent as a classic chocolate mousse but are made without cream, eggs, or chocolate. They are surprisingly rich and chocolaty, so a little goes a long way. This recipe makes four small servings—it will easily double if you're feeling greedy!

Serves 4

1 large ripe avocados
1 large ripe banana,
    peeled and chopped
¼ cup maple syrup
½ cup good-quality cocoa
    powder (I use Green &
    Blacks; check the label
    to ensure it is dairy-free),
    sifted

For the pecan brittle
Flavorless oil, for
    greasing (such as
    groundnut)
½ cup pecans
¼ cup superfine sugar
2 tablespoons maple syrup
1 tablespoon cold water
A pinch of sea salt

1. First make the chocolate pudding: Place the avocado flesh in a food processor with the chopped banana, maple syrup, cocoa, and a small pinch of salt. Pulse until smooth.

2. Spoon into four small glasses or espresso cups and refrigerate for at least 1 hour, or up to 6 hours ahead.

3. Meanwhile, make the maple pecan brittle: Line a baking sheet with parchment paper and lightly grease with a little flavorless oil. Scatter the pecans onto the pan and set aside.

4. Put the sugar, maple syrup, and cold water in a heavy-bottomed, nonstick frying pan. Heat very gently until the sugar dissolves, without stirring. This will take about 5 minutes. Allow to bubble until it turns dark golden in color. This will take another 3 to 5 minutes; the water needs to evaporate for the sugar to be able to turn to caramel (and set hard). Add the salt, then pour the caramel over the nuts. Let cool for at least 30 minutes until hard, then bash with a rolling pin to break into shards.

5. Add a few shards of pecan brittle to each chocolate pudding just before serving.

COCONUT CHOCOLATE TRUFFLES

*VEGETARIAN *DAIRY-FREE *GLUTEN-FREE

These are so simple to make and omit the saturated fat-laden heavy cream traditionally used in a chocolate ganache. Avocado adds richness and indulgence as well as lots of goodness. Play around with the toppings—try crushed pistachios, finely chopped toasted hazelnuts, or grated chocolate sprinkles.

Makes 18 to 20 truffles

4½ ounces good-quality dark chocolate (about 70 percent cocoa solids; check the label to ensure it is dairy-free), chopped
2½ tablespoons light brown sugar
½ teaspoon vanilla extract
1 small ripe avocado (you need ¾ cup flesh)
3 tablespoons coconut cream
½ cup shredded coconut, for coating

1. Slowly melt the chocolate and sugar in a heatproof bowl over a saucepan of barely simmering water. Once melted, remove from the heat and stir in the vanilla extract. Let cool for about 20 minutes.

2. Coarsely chop the avocado flesh, add to a food processor, then add the cooled chocolate mixture and coconut cream. Pulse until smooth. Scrape into a bowl and refrigerate for at least 2 hours or until firm.

3. Spread the shredded coconut out on a large plate. Take a teaspoonful of the mixture and roll into a ball, then roll in the coconut to coat. Repeat until you have used all the mixture, then transfer to a baking sheet lined with parchment paper and chill until needed. They will keep for up to 2 to 3 days in an airtight container in the fridge.

PISTACHIO & AVOCADO ICE CREAM

*VEGETARIAN *DAIRY FREE *GLUTEN-FREE

Avocado lends itself perfectly to this twist on the Italian favorite. Its vibrant green color goes hand in hand with the pistachio's natural hue and provides creaminess and richness without the need for dairy or eggs.

Serves 8 to 10
Makes 3½ cups

1 (14-ounce) can full-fat coconut milk
½ cup superfine sugar
1¼ cups shelled pistachio kernels
1 medium ripe avocado (about 1 cup)
Sea salt

1. Place the coconut milk and sugar in a saucepan. Heat very gently over low heat until the sugar dissolves—don't allow to boil. Remove from the heat. Let cool, then refrigerate for at least an hour until cold.

2. When the coconut mixture is cold, add the pistachios to a food-processor and grind to a powder. Next, add the avocado flesh, then add the coconut mixture and a pinch of salt, and blend until smooth. Taste and add a little more salt, if needed.

3. Transfer to an ice cream maker and churn for 30 to 40 minutes until very thick, then transfer to a freezer proof container (about 1 quart) and freeze for at least 4 hours, or until ready to use. If you don't have an ice cream maker, transfer the mixture to a freezer proof container and freeze for at least 8 hours, whisking every 30 minutes until solid.

If you have leftover ripe avocado, there's no need to throw it in the compost; you can freeze it. The texture of the thawed avocado won't be nice in salads, but is perfect for whizzing into smoothies and dressings or smashing into guacamole.

CHEWY CHOCOLATE HAZELNUT BROWNIES

*VEGETARIAN *DAIRY-FREE

Unctuous, chewy, and super chocolatey, these brownies taste anything but healthy. I won't pretend they are completely virtuous, but using avocado instead of butter reduces the saturated fat content (and overall calories), making these brownies less guilt-inducing than the traditional variety. It also makes them a winner for anyone who is lactose-intolerant. Share them with friends or family alongside a cup of coffee.

Serves 12 to 16

¾ cup blanched hazelnuts

5½ ounces good-quality dark chocolate (about 70 percent cocoa solids; dairy-free—check the label), chopped

¼ cup coconut oil, plus extra for greasing

3 large eggs

1 cup light brown sugar

1 teaspoon vanilla extract

1 medium–large ripe avocado (about 1 cup flesh)

¾ cup self-rising flour

⅓ cup good-quality cocoa powder (check it's dairy-free)

Sea salt

If you like mocha brownies add 2 teaspoons of instant espresso powder and swap the chunks for milk chocolate if you eat dairy.

1. Preheat the oven to 350°F. Grease and line an 8-inch square brownie pan with parchment paper. Spread the hazelnuts out in a large roasting pan and bake for 6 to 8 minutes until toasted. Set aside to cool then coarsely chop. Melt 3½ ounces of chocolate and the coconut oil in a heatproof bowl over a saucepan of barely simmering water, remove from the heat, and let cool slightly.

2. Meanwhile, pulse the eggs, sugar, and vanilla together in a food processor until combined. Add the avocado flesh and process until smooth. Transfer to a large bowl, add the cooled chocolate mixture, sift in the flour and cocoa, add a pinch of salt, then whisk everything together. Fold in most of the chopped hazelnuts and the remaining chopped chocolate.

3. Spoon into the pan and level. Scatter with the remaining chopped hazelnuts. Bake for 20 to 25 minutes until just firm to the touch. Let cool slightly in the pan before transferring to a wire rack to cool completely. Cut into squares. These are also delicious served warm with vanilla ice cream for dessert, if you can eat dairy. The cooled brownies will keep in an airtight container for up to three days

BANANA & WALNUT
BREAD *VEGETARIAN *DAIRY-FREE

Avocado is swapped in again for butter to make this a naturally dairy-free bread. It also makes it much lower in saturated fat and lower in calories than regular banana breads. Use ripe or overripe bananas for this recipe. Whenever you are left with a speckled-skinned banana that is too ripe to eat, freeze it in its skin, and defrost before using.

Serves 10

⅔ cup walnuts, coarsely chopped
½ medium ripe avocado (about ½ cup flesh)
½ cup light brown sugar
1 large egg
1 teaspoon vanilla extract
1½ cups all-purpose flour
2 teaspoons baking powder
Sea salt
3 ripe or overripe bananas (about 1¼ cups), coarsely mashed

1. Preheat the oven to 350°F. Line a nonstick 2-pound loaf pan (8 × 4 × 3 inches) with parchment paper. You can lightly grease with coconut oil if not using a nonstick pan.

2. Spread the walnuts out on a baking sheet and bake for 5 minutes. Let cool, then coarsely chop.

3. Meanwhile, put the avocado flesh, sugar, egg, and vanilla extract into a food processor. Pulse until smooth. Transfer to a large bowl.

4. Sift in the flour, baking powder, and a pinch of salt. Whisk until combined, then whisk in most of the banana until smooth. Fold in the remaining banana and most of the toasted walnuts. Spoon into the prepared pan, scatter with the rest of the walnuts, and place on a baking sheet.

5. Bake for about 1 hour, or until a skewer inserted into the middle comes out clean. You may need to return it to the oven for 5 to 10 minutes if it still seems a bit sticky in the center. Let cool in the pan for 15 minutes before transferring to a cooling rack to cool completely. The cake will keep in an airtight container for 3 to 4 days.

EQUIPMENT: THE ESSENTIALS

More often than not, there's little more than a fork or a decent, sharp cook's knife needed, but there are one or two other bits of basic equipment you might find useful.

Pestle and mortar

This is very useful for crushing garlic or spices and smashing small amounts of avocado.

A decent box grater

Ideal for grating raw carrots, beetroot or courgettes into salads and slaws. A spiralizer is great if you have the storage space, but a grater or julienne peeler does the same thing; it just takes a little more time and patience.

A fine grater

This is one of my most-used utensils, excellent for speedily grating fresh garlic and root ginger as well as cheese. I use a Microplane but there are plenty of good brands available.

A simple citrus reamer or juicer

Limes and lemons are an avocado's best friend and used in many recipes. You don't need any fancy gadgetry here, just something to help you efficiently extract juice and separate the seeds.

Mini food-processor

This is one gadget I couldn't live without. It is brilliant for making chunky purées, guacamole, pastes and whizzing into dressings. It is also great for speedily chopping onions and garlic. If you don't have one, a pestle and mortar can be used for purées and pastes, but if you spend a lot of time in the kitchen, it is a worthwhile (and affordable) investment. A handheld stick blender is also a good alternative.

Food-processor

Larger than its mini sibling (above), this is so useful for making larger quantities of guacamole or hummus. I also use it for whizzing cake mixture or making nut butter, ganache or an ice cream base. It can also be used for soups and smoothies if you don't have a blender. It often comes with lots of useful attachments, including graters, juicers, dough hooks and a smaller bowl.

High speed blender/ smoothie maker or nutri bullet

This is not an essential, but with a super sharp blade and extra power, it is excellent for giving a velvety smooth finish to soups and smoothies. A good investment if you make smoothies regularly.

Digital scales

In the savory recipes in this book, a guide is given for the size of the avocado needed, but a few grams here or there won't make much difference. For baking, however, I like to be more precise, and a set of digital scales will give you accuracy and peace of mind, which can make all the difference.

USEFUL NOTES
ON INGREDIENTS

♦ Hass avocados were used in the testing of these recipes as these are the most widely available variety, but it should be interchangeable with other varieties.

♦ All **vegetables, herbs and salad** ingredients are washed.

♦ **Garlic, onion and shallots** are peeled, unless stated otherwise.

♦ **Lemons and limes**—these vary in their juiciness, so use the amounts stated in the recipes as a general guide and add more juice to taste.

♦ **Chiles**—the heat in chiles can vary, so it's important to use these recipes as a guide and adjust to your taste, leaving in the seeds if you prefer a more intense heat level. You can always add more to boost the heat, but it's much harder to take it away!

♦ **Sea salt**—I prefer to use a natural sea or rock salt for a better flavor. Fine table salt often contains anti-caking agents to prevent the crystals from sticking together.

♦ **Meat, fish and eggs**—buy the best you can afford, ideally they should be sustainably sourced and free range.

♦ **Seasoning**—this is very much down to personal taste, so I have only specified an amount of salt where I think it is essential to a recipe. For the rest of the recipes, add as much or as little as you like to suit your palette.

How to freeze leftover avocado
There are two main ways to freeze avocado:

As a purée: whizz in a mini food-processor with a little lemon or lime juice, then transfer to a freezer bag and label, or fill up ice cube trays.

As halves: halve, pit and peel the avocado, sprinkle with a little lemon juice, wrap tightly in plastic wrap, then place in a freezer bag, seal, and freeze. Defrost before using. Defrost before using in smoothies, dressings, or dips.

Weights and measures
All teaspoon and tablespoon measures are level.
All avocados are halved, pitted, and peeled before use.
Average weight of an avocado (flesh only):
Large—200g
Medium—150–175g
Small—125g

INDEX

ACKNOWLEDGMENTS

Heaps of ideas, countless tests, masses of photographs and possibly hundreds of avocados later and the book is complete, well, almost. First, there are a few very important thank yous to be said.

My first big thank you has to be to Kyle for giving me the opportunity to write my début cookbook. I'm so grateful to have had the chance to write 40 recipes using an ingredient which I genuinely ADORE. I've loved every part of the process, so thank you.

I'd also like to say a big thank you to the rest of the team at Kyle Books; I really do appreciate all of the hard work that goes on behind the scenes; your attention to detail and quest for perfection is second to none. In particular to Vicky, for initially helping me turn the idea into a reality, and to Claire for your patience, advice and support throughout. And a big thank you to Helen for sprinkling your design magic and sewing the chapters together so beautifully.

I'm incredibly lucky to have worked with such a fantastic and talented team—a great deal of hard work went into the photoshoots, so I owe special thanks to all of those who made these days a joy as well as a success.

To Clare—what can I say? Your beautiful photography is an inspiration, and I am in total awe of how you make such a skill appear so effortless. I've so enjoyed our shoots; your "nothing is too much trouble" attitude, unshakeable composure and sense of humor were invaluable.

Wei, thank you for bringing your unique touch and unquashable enthusiasm to this project. Your fabulous props are always just right—and, as always, you are so lovely to work with.

Jenna, thank you for loving avocados as much as I do, and for all your hard work. You are a wonderful cook.

Finally, to my family, for your love, unwavering support and interest in all of my work. This means the world to me. And lastly, but by no means least, to Ian for putting up with my avocado "tunnel vision" for a good few months and for remaining excited about your fifth avocado-based meal of a weekend. Thank you for your honesty and exacting tastebuds, but, most of all, thank you for challenging, inspiring and believing in me.

Published in 2016 by Kyle Books
www.kylebooks.com

Distributed by National Book Network
4501 Forbes Blvd, Suite 200,
Lanham, MD 20706
Phone: (800) 462-6420
Fax: (800) 338-4550
customercare@nbnbooks.com

10 9 8 7 6 5 4 3 2

ISBN 978-1-909487-54-3

Project Editor: Claire Rogers
Copy Editor: Eve Pertile
Designer: Helen Bratby
Photographer: Clare Winfield
Illustrator: Jenni Desmond
Food Stylist: Lucy Jessop
Food Stylist's Assistant: Jenna Leiter
Prop Stylist: Wei Tang
Production: Nic Jones and Gemma John

Library of Congress Control Number:
2016939821

Color reproduction by ALTA London
Printed and bound in China by C&C Offset
Printing Co., Ltd.

* Note: all eggs are free-range